Global
Business English

CONTENTS

PART
2   Business English Communication

PART 1

For Business Trip

01 Chapter Reservation

Key Words & Phrases

- reserve/book
- available

- accept
- land/ landing

- immigrate/ immigration
- certainly

- charge
- employee

- passport
- provide

- booking process
- passport

- conveyor belt
- empty

- single room/ double room/ suite room/ twin room

Useful Expressions

1. I want to reserve a room.

2. When do you plan to check in?

3. Hold the line, please.

4. We have a single room available on that day.

5. Your reservation is done.

6. I am sorry but we are fully booked today.

7. Thank you for your understanding.

8. Would you sign here, ma'am?

9. Did you have a reservation?

10. May I have your passport?/ Here you are.

11. How long are you going to stay here?

12. Where will you be staying?

11. What's the purpose of your visit?

12. Enjoy your stay.

13. Do you accept American Express card?

14. Have a good trip.

15. I'll take it.

D Dialogue 1   Reservation

 Reservation Guest

Good morning, Hilton Hotel. How can I help you?

I want to reserve a single room with a bath for two nights.

Certainly, sir. When do you plan to check in?

May 2nd.

Hold the line, please. I'll check on that.
We have a single room available on that day.

How much do you charge for a single room?

The room charge is $100 per night.

OK. I will take it.

What name is it under?

Ji Soo Leem.

All right. Your reservation is done. Thank you for calling.

Dialogue 2   **Check in**

 Front Desk   Guest

 Welcome to Western Hotel. May I help you?

I'd like to check in.

Did you have a reservation?

Yes. My name is Ji Soo Leem and I have a reservation for two nights.

Oh, I am sorry but we are fully booked today.

No rooms? I made a reservation a few weeks ago.

Whose name was it under?

Ji Soo Leem.

I'll check on that again. Oh, here is a memo about your reservation.
But our employee missed your name in the booking process. We will
provide you a suite room. You can stay at the same price.

OK. I'll take it.

Thank you for your understanding.

Dialogue 3   Flight Reservation and Ticketing for Business Trip

 Staff   Passenger

Good afternoon, ma'am? How may I help you?

Yes, I made a reservation for a flight to L.A. on Saturday.

May I have your name?

My name is Miss Leem.

You are going to L.A. Asiana 707, business class, right?

Yes, right. Do you accept American Express card?

Sure, may I have your credit card and passport, please?

Here you are.

Would you sign here, ma'am?

Sure.

Thank you. Have a good trip.

Thank you, Bye!

Dialogue 4   Landing and Immigration

 Inspection 1   Passenger   Inspection 2

May I have your passport?

Here you are.

Please put all your bags on the conveyor.
And then step right this way, ma'am.
(Beep)
Please empty your pockets and go through again.

Thank you.

-Immigration Office-

May I have your passport?

Here you are.

How long are you going to stay here?

Maybe for about two weeks.

Where will you be staying?

At the Hilton Hotel.

What's the purpose of your visit?

For business trip.

OK. Here is your passport. Enjoy your stay.

Thank you. Good bye.

✿ Fill in the blanks with proper words.

| purpose | for | here you are | where | long |

-Immigration Office-

May I have your passport?

_____.

How _____ are you going to stay here?

Maybe for about two weeks.

_____ will you be staying?

At the Hilton Hotel.

What's the _____ of your visit?

_____ business trip.

OK. Here is your passport. Enjoy your stay.

Thank you. Good bye.

Comprehension Check-up

Answer the following sentences.

1. Did you have a reservation?

   ⇨ _____

2. When do you plan to check in?

   ⇨ _____

3. How long are you going to stay here?

   ⇨ _____

4. What's the purpose of your visit?

   ⇨ _____

5. How much do you charge for a single room?

   ⇨ _____

6. What name is it under?

   ⇨ _____

7. Where will you be staying?

   ⇨ _____.

Translation

Translate the following sentences into English.

1. 싱글룸 하나를 예약하고 싶습니다.

   ⇨ _____

2. 당신의 예약이 완료되었습니다.

   ⇨ _____

3. 오늘은 예약이 꽉 찼습니다.

   ⇨ _____

4. 이해해 주셔서 감사합니다.

   ⇨ _____

5. 여기에 싸인 해 주시겠습니까?

   ⇨ _____

6. 여권 좀 볼 수 있을까요?

   ⇨ _____

Exercise 1

1. The bus tickets are _____ on request.

(A) portable　　　　　　　　(B) useful

(C) available　　　　　　　　(D) flexible

2. I would like to _____ a table for five people.

(A) reserve　　　　　　　　　(B) preserve

(C) conserve　　　　　　　　(D) observe

3. I was sorry that I could not _____ your invitation yesterday.

(A) assist　　　　　　　　　　(B) allow

(C) accept　　　　　　　　　　(D) access

4. We will be _____ soon. Please fasten your seatbelt.

(A) landing　　　　　　　　　(B) lending

(C) loading　　　　　　　　　(D) interesting

5. Would you fill in all the blanks on this _____ form?

(A) uniform　　　　　　　　　(B) immigration

(C) destination　　　　　　　(D) baggage claim

6. A lot of people _____ that if scientists develop AI robot, there will be many problems.

(A) believes

(B) believe

(C) are believed

(D) to believe

7. Henry is very _____, friendly, and polite.

(A) kindness

(B) kindly

(C) kindliness

(D) kind

8. Mary wants to hire a person _____ good at speaking English.

(A) whose are

(B) who are

(C) whose is

(D) who is

9. Sam, a teacher, _____ write letters to his students.

(A) is

(B) are

(C) is going to

(D) are going to

10. Many students with good skills _____ difficulty solving problems.

(A) are having

(B) is having

(C) has

(D) are doing

Answer

1. C   2. A   3. C   4. A   5. B   6. B   7. D   8. D   9. C   10. A

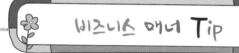 비즈니스 매너 **Tip**

 악수할 때 1

악수방법은

🍃 상대방의 눈을 쳐다보면서

🍃 바른 자세와 밝은 표정을 지으면서

🍃 오른손으로 살짝 힘 있게 3회 정도 흔들며

🍃 인사말과 함께한다.

🍃 손가락 끝으로 성의 없이하거나 지나치게 세게 잡지 않는다.

Asking Direction and Information

Key Words & Phrases

- direction
- information

- recommend
- expensive

- rate
- subway

- convention
- cross

- miss
- in the middle of 30's

- third floor

- cosmetic

- take A to B

Useful Expressions

1. Could you recommend a Business Hotel?

2. Not too expensive.

3. Could you tell me how to get to Kookje University?

4. Is there any other way to get there?

5. Cross the street and keep walking down.

6. You can't miss it.

7. You can go there by taxi.

8. Where are you coming from?

9. I would like to come by subway.

10. How far is it?

11. It is not that far.

12. It takes 10 minutes by bus.

13. Thank you for your kindness.

14. Where do you want to go first?

15. Can I ask you why?

16. I would like to buy a gift for my wife.

17. She is in the middle of 30's.

D Dialogue 1   Information Desk ①

Information Desk Clerk   Passenger

Good morning, sir. May I help you?

Good morning, could you recommend a Business Hotel?

Not too expensive.

A bed and breakfast will be all right.

How long will you stay?

For a week, I guess.

All right, sir. Here is a brochure with all the rates of hotels.

Oh, that's good. Thank you.

Have a good trip!

Dialogue 2 — Information Desk ②

 Information Desk Clerk Passenger

Information desk. May I help you?

Yes. Could you tell me how to get to Kookje University?

Where are you coming from?

From Seoul. I'd like to come by subway.

Then take the Subway Line 1 to Seojungri Station.

And Kookje shuttle bus will come every 10 minutes in front of the

station.

How far is it?

It is not that far. It takes 10 minutes by bus.

I see. Thank you for your kindness.

My pleasure.

Dialogue 3　Directions

😊 Information Desk Clerk　😎 Passenger

😎 Excuse me. I am looking for Kookje convention center.

Could you tell me how to get there?

😊 No problem, sir. Cross the street and keep walking down a few blocks.

Then, you can't miss it. It is on your left.

😎 Is there any other way to get there?

😊 You can go there by taxi.

The taxi stop is in front of Seojungri Station.

😎 Thank you so much.

😊 You're welcome.

Dialogue 4 Information

 Travel Agent Client

Where do you want to go first?

Can you take me to the department store?

Can I ask you why?

I'd like to buy a gift for my wife.

How old is she?

She is in the middle of 30's.

I think you can find some cosmetic shops in the third floor.
I'll take you to a shopping mall.

Thank you so much.

Fill in the blanks with proper words.

| it is not that far | in front of | my pleasure | how to get to | take |

Information Desk. May I help you?

Yes. Could you tell me _____ Kookje University?

Where are you coming from?

From Seoul. I'd like to come by subway.

Then _____ the Subway Line 1 to Seojungri Station.

And Kookje shuttle bus will come every 10 minutes

_____the station.

How far is it?

_____. It takes 10 minutes by bus.

I see. Thank you for your kindness.

_____.

Comprehension Check-up

 Answer the following sentences.

1. Could you tell me how to get to Kookje University?

   ⇨ _____

2. Is there any other way to get there?

   ⇨ _____

3. Where do you want to go first?

   ⇨ _____

4. How far is it?

   ⇨ _____

5. Where are you coming from?

   ⇨ _____

6. Can I ask you why?

   ⇨ _____

7. I'd like to buy a gift for my wife.

   ⇨ _____

Translation

Translate the following sentences into English.

1. 택시로 가시면 됩니다.

    ⇨ _____

2. 그렇게 멀지는 않아요.

    ⇨ _____

3. 버스로 10분 걸립니다.

    ⇨ _____

4. 그 도로를 가로질러서 계속 내려가시면 됩니다.

    ⇨ _____

5. 그녀는 30대 중반입니다.

    ⇨ _____

6. 좋은 호텔을 추천해주시겠습니까?

    ⇨ _____

Exercise 2

1. Could you _____ a famous tourist spot for me?

   (A) recommend   (B) commend

   (C) stop   (D) know

2. The room _____ at the hotel includes dinner fee for this Christmas season.

   (A) signature   (B) rate

   (C) sign   (D) race

3. I know this necktie is _____, but I really want to take it as a gift for my husband.

   (A) expansive   (B) heavy

   (C) expensive   (D) dirty

4. Does the shuttle bus _____ me to Seojungri Station?

   (A) keep   (B) see

   (C) give   (D) take

5. She wants to go a _____ shop to buy eye liners.

   (A) cosmetic   (B) shoe

   (C) dress   (D) coffee

6. BTS is one of _____ singers in South Korea.

  (A) the most famous   (B) famously

  (C) more famous   (D) almost famous

7. Which is _____ month of the year?

  (A) more hot   (B) most hotter

  (C) as hot as   (D) the hottest

8. Smart phones are _____ than the other electronic devices.

  (A) more usefully   (B) more useful

  (C) as useful   (D) as useful as

9. The Jeonju international film festival will be delayed _____ it rains tomorrow morning.

  (A) unless   (B) if

  (C) had   (D) otherwise

10. If I move back to Texas, I _____ your family very much.

  (A) will be missing   (B) missed

  (C) will miss   (D) would miss

Answer

1. A   2. B   3. C   4. D   5. A   6. A   7. D   8. B   9. B   10. C

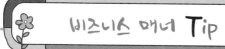

악수할 때 2

손을 먼저 내미는 사람은

🌿 손윗사람이 손아랫사람에게,

🌿 여성이 남성에게,

🌿 기혼자가 미혼자에게,

🌿 상급자가 하급자에게 손을 내밀어서 하는 것이 좋다.

03 Ordering Food

Key Words & Phrases

- tray table
- meal
- meat
- all together
- preference
- absolutely
- non-smoking section
- today's special
- medium well-done
- anything else
- order potato fries
- option

Useful Expressions

1. We'll be serving lunch soon.

2. What's the meal today?

3. What would you like to drink?

4. Here you are.

5. Enjoy your meal.

6. I'd like to reserve a table.

7. What time will it be?

8. How many people are there in your party?

9. Do you have any seating preference?

10. What is today's special?

11. How about the steak?

12. How would you like your steak?

13. I'll be right back with your order.

14. Would you like to order?

15. What are the options?

16. Here is your order.

D Dialogue 1   In the Cabin

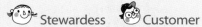 Stewardess   Customer

Excuse me, sir. We'll be serving lunch soon. Would you mind opening your tray table?

Sure, what's the meal today?

We have Korean style Bibimbab and meat with rice.

Meat with rice, please.

What would you like to drink?

We have coffee, orange juice, and water.

Just water, please.

Here you are. Enjoy your meal, sir.

D Dialogue 2 In the Restaurant

Waiter   **Guest**

Good morning, Kookje Restaurant. May I help you?

I'd like to reserve a table for Saturday evening.

All right. What time will it be, ma'am?

At 6:30 p.m.

Certainly, ma'am. How many people are there in your party?

Six all together.

Do you have any seating preference?

Yes, can I have non-smoking section, please? Because of my child.

Absolutely, ma'am.

D Dialogue 3　Ordering Steak

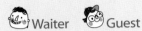 Waiter　 Guest

Good afternoon, sir. Here is the menu.

Thank you. What is today's special?

How about the steak?

Good. I'll have it.

How would you like your steak?

Medium well-done, please.

Anything else? Would you like something to drink?

I'd like some red wine.

Okay. I'll be right back with your order.

Dialogue 4 Ordering Hamburger

 Clerk Guest

Would you like to order?

Can I get the cheese burger, please?

Would you like the burger with some tomatoes in the middle?

Yes, please.

And the fries with it, too?

I want sweet potato fries but do you have other options?

We have boiled brocoli or salad.

Then, I'll have salad.

Okay. Here is your order.

✿ Fill in the blanks with proper words.

| how would you like   to drink   right back   special   well-done |

Good afternoon, sir. Here is the menu.

Thank you. What is today's _____?

How about the steak?

Good. I'll have it.

_____ your steak?

Medium _____, please.

Anything else? Would you like something _____?

I'd like some red wine.

Okay. I'll be _____ with your order.

Comprehension Check-up

 Answer the following sentences.

1. What would you like to drink?

    ⇨ _____

2. What's the meal today?

    ⇨ _____

3. How many people are there in your party?

    ⇨ _____

4. How would you like your steak?

    ⇨ _____

5. Would you like something to drink?

    ⇨ _____

6. Would you like to order?

    ⇨ _____

7. What are the options?

    ⇨ _____

Translation

Translate the following sentences into English.

1. 어떤 것을 마시겠습니까?

   ⇨ _____

2. 즐거운 식사 되십시오.

   ⇨ _____

3. 몇 명이십니까?

   ⇨ _____

4. 금연구역으로 해주세요.

   ⇨ _____

5. 스테이크 굽기는 어느 정도로 해드릴까요?

   ⇨ _____

6. 주문하시겠습니까?

   ⇨ _____

Exercise 3

1. I _____ vegetables to meat.

   (A) like   (B) hate

   (C) prefer   (D) have

2. They are _____ chicken over the phone.

   (A) eating   (B) ordering

   (C) completing   (D) coming

3. Getting a job is not a(n) _____ for me.

   (A) option   (B) position

   (C) competition   (D) section

4. I think you need to ask the _____ in a grocery store.

   (A) waiter   (B) chef

   (C) doctor   (D) clerk

5. Uni knows that it is a special book, _____.

   (A) shortly   (B) lately

   (C) extremely   (D) absolutely

6. Tobacco is the second _____ cause of death in the world.

   (A) more bigger   (B) much bigger

   (C) biggest   (D) the most biggest

7. The deployment of the THAAD is always a difficult and _____ _____ issue.

   (A) positive   (B) sensitive

   (C) attractive   (D) sensible

8. _____ getting a bonus, all workers will go Taiwan for the vacation.

   (A) In addition to   (B) As a result

   (C) Due to   (D) In spite of

9. Jocelyn will participate in the conference _____ the day.

   (A) through   (B) for

   (C) throughout   (D) cross

10. _____ heavy rain, all flights are delayed or canceled.

   (A) Because   (B) Because of

   (C) Since   (D) While

Answer

1. C   2. B   3. A   4. D   5. D   6. C   7. B   8. A   9. C   10. B

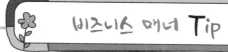

비즈니스 매너 Tip

명함 교환할 때 1

명함 줄 때

🌿 일어서서 두 손으로

🌿 상대방이 읽을 수 있는 방향으로

🌿 가슴과 허리선 사이에서

🌿 명함을 내밀 때 인사말과 함께 자신을 소개하면서

🌿 공손하게 건넨다.

Local Tour
(Rent a Car, Lost and Found, Health Trouble, Bank)

Key Words & Phrases

- be supposed to
- sore ankle
- make it worse
- missing
- leave
- consulate
- issue
- pamphlet
- be interested in
- rate
- charge
- form
- international driver's license
- fill out

Useful Expressions

1. I am supposed to go to the walking tour of the city.

2. What's the problem?

3. I have a sore ankle and I don't want to make it worse.

4. Would that be better?

5. Where did you leave it?

6. It's gone now.

7. What's in it?

8. The first thing you have to do is to contact the police.

9. What about the passport and my plane ticket?

10. You have to call the consulate.

11. They will issue another ticket.

12. I'd like to rent a car.

13. We have all kinds of cars.

14. Gas is on you.

15. Just sign here.

16. Please fill out this form.

D Dialogue 1 Changing Tour

 Tourist    Tour Guide

Hello! I am supposed to go to the walking tour today, but I won't be able to go.

That's too bad. What's the problem?

I have a sore ankle and I don't want to make it worse.

Well, you can change to the taxi tour if you want.
Would that be better?

That would be fine.

Dialogue 2   Missing

Tourist   Guide

I can't see my bag anywhere. I've looked everywhere, but it's missing.

Where did you leave it?

I just put it on the chair a few minutes ago. But it's gone now.

What's in it?

Well, my credit card, my passport and plane ticket.
I guess someone stole it.

The first thing you have to do is to contact the police.

What about the passport and my plane ticket?

You have to call the consulate. And you need to call the airline and
explain what happened. I'm sure they will issue another ticket.

I see. Thank you!

Dialogue 3   Rent a Car

 Rental Clerk   Guest

May I help you?

Yes, I'd like to rent a car. May I see your pamphlet?

Sure. Here you are. We have all kinds of cars. What type of car are you interested in?

Mid size. What's the rate?

We charge $100 for midsize. But gas is on you.

Okay, I will take it.

Can I see your passport, an international driver's license and a credit card?

Here you are.

Just sign here and take this key.

Thank you.

Have a good trip.

D Dialogue 4 At the Bank

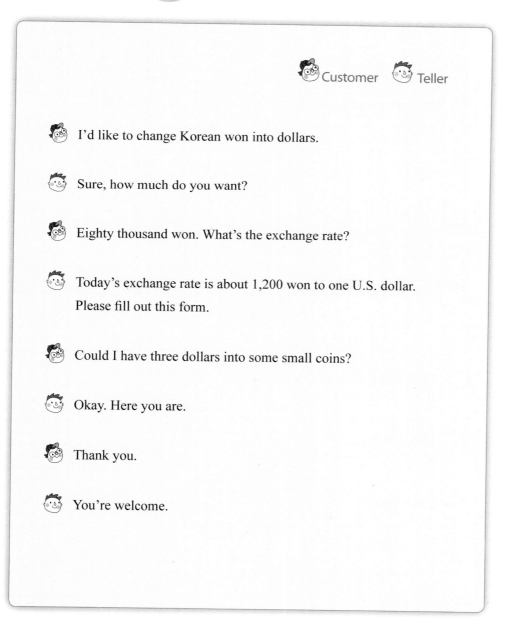

Customer Teller

I'd like to change Korean won into dollars.

Sure, how much do you want?

Eighty thousand won. What's the exchange rate?

Today's exchange rate is about 1,200 won to one U.S. dollar.
Please fill out this form.

Could I have three dollars into some small coins?

Okay. Here you are.

Thank you.

You're welcome.

✿ Fill in the blanks with proper words.

| rate | fill out | you are welcome | into | how much |

I'd like to change Korean won _____ dollars.

Sure, _____ do you want?

Eighty thousand won. What's the exchange _____?

Today's exchange rate is about 1,200 won to one U.S. dollar. Please _____ this form.

Could I have three dollars into some small coins?

Okay. Here you are.

Thank you.

_____.

Comprehension Check-up

Answer the following sentences.

1. What's the problem?

   _____

2. Would that be better?

   _____

3. Where did you leave it?

   _____

4. What type of car are you interested in?

   _____

5. What's the rate?

   _____

6. What's the exchange rate?

   _____

45

Translation

Translate the following sentences into English.

1. 오늘 도보여행하려고 했는데, 할 수 없을 것 같아요.

    ⇨ _____

2. 무엇이 문제인가요?

    ⇨ _____

3. 어디에 놓고 왔나요?

    ⇨ _____

4. 그 안에 무엇이 들어있나요?

    ⇨ _____

5. 연료는 당신이 부담해야합니다.

    ⇨ _____

6. 이 양식을 작성해주세요.

    ⇨ _____

Exercise 4

1. What is _____, Jin lost his wallet.

   (A) bad   (B) worse

   (C) worst   (D) more worse

2. We tried to _____ with the embassy by phone but we could not.

   (A) contract   (B) contact

   (C) consider   (D) sound

3. What is offered to customers at no _____ is breakfast.

   (A) discharge   (B) charge

   (C) attack   (D) order

4. You need a _____ to go to another country.

   (A) bill   (B) passenger

   (C) pass   (D) passport

5. South Korea plans to _____ special stamp to celebrate Pyeongchang Olympic.

   (A) issue   (B) remain

   (C) topic   (D) miss

6. Josh went to school _____ he caught a cold yesterday.

   (A) because   (B) by

   (C) even though   (D) regarding

7. Linda was good student and _____ along with her friends well.

   (A) gets   (B) has gotten

   (C) will get   (D) got

8. Jane is a hard _____ person with a good skill.

   (A) working   (B) to work

   (C) work   (D) being worked

9. The movie was very _____, so we fell asleep.

   (A) bore   (B) bored

   (C) boring   (D) being bored

10. _____ no money, I cannot buy that lovely house.

   (A) Having   (B) Had

   (C) If having   (D) Have

Answer

1. B   2. B   3. B   4. D   5. A   6. C   7. D   8. A   9. C   10. A

비즈니스 매너 Tip

명함 교환할 때 2

명함 받을 때

🌿 일어서서 가볍게 인사하며 두 손으로 공손하게 받는다.

🌿 동시에 교환하는 경우는 오른손으로 주고 왼손으로 받는다.

🌿 받은 명함의 내용을 확인하면서 상대에게 관심을 표현하고

🌿 읽기 어려운 글자는 그 자리에서 정중하게 물어본다.

🌿 받은 명함은 구기거나 부채질을 하는 등 함부로 다루지 않고 소중하게 다룬다.

🌿 받은 명함은 책상 위 자신이 보기 좋은 곳에 놓고 참고하면서 대화한다.

🌿 헤어질 때는 명함을 잊지 않고 가지고 간다.

Shopping

Key Words & Phrases

- quite
- rage
- try on
- fitting room
- certainly
- suit
- include
- reasonable
- excellent
- expensive
- newest
- look around
- mid-forties
- solid
- trendy
- loud
- nowadays
- exchangeable
- refundable
- wrap
- payment
- receipt

Useful Expressions

1. Why don't you try it on?

2. Do you have anything blue?

3. Where is the fitting room?

4. I am looking for some trousers.

5. What size do you want?

6. Do you think this suits me?

7. It looks good on you.

8. It's quite resonable.

9. Is there anything I can help you?

10. Can you show me a mobile phone?

11. What make do you want?

12. I'm looking for a gift for my wife.

13. May I ask her age?

14. How about this scarf?

15. Do you have anything not too loud?

16. Can I exchange it?

17. It is exchangeable and refundable.

18. Wrap for a gift, please.

19. How would you like the payment?

Dialogue 1　At a Shop ①

 Clerk　 Customer

Hello. Welcome to Forever 21. May I help you?

Yes. I am looking for T-Shirts.

This red shirt is quite the rage. Why don't you try it on?

But I think it is a little loud for me. Do you have anything blue?

How about this one? This sky-blue is brand new.

Okay. Where is the fitting room?

Right this way, please.

D **Dialogue 2** **At a Shop** ②

 Clerk   Customer

Hello. How may I help you?

I am looking for some trousers.

What size so you want?

A 26 waist. Can I try it on?

Certainly, ma'am.

Do you think this suits me?

It looks good on you.

How much is it?

It comes to $30 including tax.

It's quite reasonable. I will take this one.

Dialogue 3   At a Shop ③

 Clerk   Customer

Good afternoon, is there anything I can help you?

Yes. Can you show me a mobile phone?

Certainly, sir. What make of phone do you want?

I'd like to have Samsung Galaxy.

This phone is very excellent, but it is not expensive.

I am looking for the newest one.

Then, how about this Galaxy Note? It is the newest one.

Umm... after looking around more, I will choose one.

Okay. Take your time.

Dialogue 4 **At a Shop** ④

 Clerk  Customer

Good afternoon, sir. May I help you?

I'm looking for a gift for my wife.

May I ask her age?

She is in mid-forties.

Oh, I see. How about this scarf?
It is new arrivals.

But it's solid pink! Do you have anything not too loud?

Sir, this is very trendy colors nowadays.

I see. But in case my wife does not like it, can I exchange it?

Of course. It is exchangeable and refundable.

Then wrap for a gift, please.

How would you like the payment? By credit card or in cash?

Credit card, please.

OK, here you are.

Here's your receipt and the card.

Thank you.

Good bye.

✿ Fill in the blanks with proper words.

| looks good | suits | reasonable | try | looking for |

Hello. How may I help you?

I am _____ some trousers.

What size so you want?

A 26 waist. Can I _____ it on?

Certainly, ma'am.

Do you think this _____ me?

It _____ on you.

How much is it?

It comes to $30 including tax.

It's quite _____. I will take this one.

Comprehension Check-up

⚙ Answer the following sentences.

1. Why don't you try it on?

    ⇨ _____

2. Where is the fitting room?

    ⇨ _____

3. What size do you want?

    ⇨ _____

4. Do you think this suits me?

    ⇨ _____

5. What make do you want?

    ⇨ _____

6. May I ask her age?

    ⇨ _____

7. How would you like the payment?

    ⇨ _____.

Translation

※ Translate the following sentences into English.

1. 적당한 가격이네요.

   ⇨ _____

2. 바지를 사려고 둘러보고 있습니다.

   ⇨ _____

3. 잘 어울리시네요.

   ⇨ _____

4. 아내를 위한 선물을 찾고 있습니다.

   ⇨ _____

5. 차분한 옷이 있습니까?

   ⇨ _____

6. 포장해주세요.

   ⇨ _____

7. 계산은 어떻게 해드릴까요?

   ⇨ _____

Exercise 5

1. Our store sells good quality products at _____ prices.

   (A) responsible   (B) reasonable

   (C) reason   (D) average

2. _____ phone of all people in this conference needs to be
   turned off.

   (A) Hand   (B) Automobile

   (C) Photo   (D) Mobile

3. But it is _____ pink! Do you have anything not too loud?

   (A) liquid   (B) beautiful

   (C) solid   (D) good

4. How about _____ our phone numbers next time?

   (A) expressing   (B) exchanging

   (C) explaining   (D) exercising

5. If you want to get information about tax _____, please
   contact the customer service.

   (A) refund   (B) soon

   (C) new   (D) turn

6. _____, learning English is very hard to me.

(A) Frankly speaking

(B) Frankly speak

(C) Frankly to speak

(D) I speaking frankly

7. What is the name of the man _____ drum on the stage?

(A) to play

(B) plays

(C) playing

(D) played

8. My family _____ Spain next year.

(A) have visited

(B) visited

(C) to visit

(D) will visit

9. I believed that Ji Yun _____ born in 1998.

(A) been

(B) being

(C) is

(D) was

10. Yoon usually _____ to her school by bus.

(A) gone

(B) goes

(C) is going

(D) go

Answer

1. B   2. D   3. C   4. B   5. A   6. A   7. C   8. D   9. D   10. B

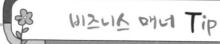

전화예절 1

전화 받을 때

🌿 전화 응대의 핵심 point는 신속, 친절, 정확이라고 할 수 있다.

🌿 벨이 2~3회 울리면 신속히 받는다.

🌿 자신의 소속과 이름을 밝힌다.

🌿 상대를 확인 후 인사한다.

🌿 용건을 잘 듣고 메모한다.

🌿 전화번호, 시간, 내용 등 주요내용을 확인한다.

🌿 마무리 인사를 한 후 상대가 수화기를 내려놓은 다음 수화기를 내려놓는다.

06 Phone Call

Key Words & Phrases

- rent
- break down
- highway
- transfer
- maintenance
- put through
- hold on
- secretarial department
- extension
- directly
- expect
- exactly
- as soon as possible
- appointment
- speaking
- regarding
- convenient

Useful Expressions

1. What's the problem?

2. It broke down on the highway.

3. I will transfer you to maintenance.

4. I'll put you through to my manager.

5. Hold on, please.

6. May I speak to Mr. Kim?

7. Who's calling please?

8. His line is busy at the moment.

9. You can speak to him directly.

10. Is this Kookje company?

11. I wish to speak to Miss Jeong.

12. She is just stepped out for lunch.

13. What time is she expected back?

14. Shall I take your message?

15. I will give her your message.

16. I am calling regarding your message.

17. When would be convenient for you?

18. It's good for me.

19. Let's see you on that day.

Dialogue 1 — At the Rental Office

Rental clerk Customer

Good morning. How may I help?

I'am calling about the car you rented me.

What's the problem?

It broke down on the highway.

Oh, I am sorry. Wait a second and I will transfer you to talk to your maintenance.

No, I want to talk to your manager.
I just want a new car right now.

All right, sir. I'll put you through to my manager.
Hold on, please.

Dialogue 2 At the Secretarial Department

 Secretary Guest

Hello! Secretarial department, Miss Jeong speaking.
How may I help you?

Hello! May I speak to Mr. Kim?

Who's calling, please?

This is Robert Brown from Samsung company.

Hold the line, please....
I'am sorry but his line is busy at the moment.
His extension number is 0087. You can speak to him directly.

Thank you.

D Dialogue 3 At a Company

Operator   Guest

Hello! Is this Kookje company?

Yes, it is.

I wish to speak to Miss Jeong.

I'm sorry, but she is just stepped out for lunch.

What time is she expected to be back?

I don't know exactly. Shall I take your message?

Could you ask her to call me back as soon as possible?

Yes, of course. May I have your name and phone number?

My name is Leem and phone number is 010-9880-1234.

Thank you for calling. I will give her your message when she comes back.

Thank you.

D Dialogue 4 Making an Appointment

Man Woman

Hello! May I speak to Miss Kim?

Yes. This is she. Speaking.

This is Mr. Han. I am calling regarding your message.

Yes, Mr. Han. I called you to see if we can change our appointment.

When would be convenient for you?

Is it possible to see you on this Saturday?

Let's see. It's good for me.

Then let's see you on that day.

✿ Fill in the blanks with proper words.

as soon as possible	stepped out	calling	shall I take	back

Hello! Is this Kookje company?

Yes, it is.

I wish to speak to Miss Jeong.

I'm sorry, but she is just _____ for lunch.

What time is she expected to be _____?

I don't know exactly. _____ your message?

Could you ask her to call me back _____?

Yes, of course. May I have your name and phone number?

My name is Leem and phone number is 010-9880-1234.

Thank you for _____. I will give her your message when she comes back.

Thank you.

Comprehension Check-up

 Answer the following sentences.

1. What's the problem?

   ⇨ _____

2. Who's calling, please?

   ⇨ _____

3. What time is she expected to be back?

   ⇨ _____

4. Shall I take your message?

   ⇨ _____

5. When would be convenient for you?

   ⇨ _____

6. I am calling regarding your message.

   ⇨ _____

Translation

Translate the following sentences into English.

1. 고속도로에서 차가 고장났어요.

   ⇨ _____

2. 제가 유지보수팀과 연결해드릴게요.

   ⇨ _____

3. 잠시만 기다려주세요.

   ⇨ _____

4. 지금 전화하신분이 누구십니까?

   ⇨ _____

5. 그녀가 언제 돌아오나요?

   ⇨ _____

6. 메시지를 남겨드릴까요?

   ⇨ _____

7. 언제가 편하신가요?

   ⇨ _____

Exercise 6

1. I am calling about the car you _____ me a few days ago.

   (A) rented   (B) landed

   (C) read   (D) booked

2. The escalator suddenly _____. We need to fix it as soon as possible.

   (A) broke down   (B) broke out

   (C) broke away   (D) broke up

3. You need to _____ to a flight to New Jersey at Dallas.

   (A) travel   (B) trade

   (C) transfer   (D) trap

4. 7-Eleven is the closest _____ store that you can find around the building.

   (A) transport   (B) inconvenient

   (C) cheap   (D) convenient

5. Let's hurry a bit. I don't want to be late for important _____ _____ because of traffic jam.

   (A) appoint   (B) point

   (C) appointment   (D) post

6. Last night, Mary _____ her sister several times.

(A) will text   (B) texted

(C) has texted   (D) text

7. All things _____, she is the best actress.

(A) considered   (B) considering

(C) to consider   (D) consider

8. Let me _____ myself.

(A) to introduce   (B) introducing

(C) introduce   (D) having introducing

9. Smoking in public places should not be _____.

(A) allow   (B) to allow

(C) having allowed   (D) allowed

10. I am looking forward _____ you again.

(A) to see   (B) to seeing

(C) for seeing   (D) in meeting

Answer

1. A   2. A   3. C   4. D   5. C   6. B   7. A   8. C   9. D   10. B

비즈니스 매너 Tip

전화예절 2

전화걸 때

🌿 전화걸기 전 용건을 미리 준비해둔다.

🌿 자신의 소속과 이름을 밝히고 상대를 확인한다.

🌿 간단한 인사를 하고 용건을 간략하게 한다.

🌿 용건이 끝나면 인사하고 마무리한다.

🌿 잘못 걸렸을 때는 정중히 사과한다.

🌿 거는 쪽이 먼저 끊는 것이 원칙이나 윗사람한테는 나중에 끊는다.

Reception

Key Words & Phrases

- reception
- make an appointment
- have a seat
- something to drink
- get on
- insurance
- product
- available
- business card
- hand to
- wake-up call
- external call
- outside line

Useful Expressions

1. Did you make an appointment?

2. Please have a seat.

3. She will be with you.

4. Coffee with cream and sugar.

5. Mr. Brown is expecting you.

6. I'll take you up to his office.

7. Would you get on the elevator?

8. May I ask your name?

9. May I ask you why?

10. Please make an appointment before you visit.

11. Here is my business card.

12. Would you give me a wake-up call at six?

13. Enjoy your stay.

D Dialogue 1　At an Office ①

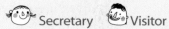 Secretary　 Visitor

How may I help you?

I'm Julie from Mirae company. I'd like to see Ms. Jeong in the Marketing Department.

Did you make an appointment?

Yes, I did.

Please have a seat and wait a moment. She will be with you in a few minutes. Would you like something to drink?

Yes, coffee with cream and sugar.

Dialogue 2 At an Office ②

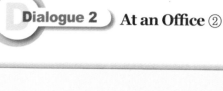
Secretary Guest CEO

Good morning. May I help you?

Good morning. I have an appointment with Mr. Brown.

Are you Miss Kim from Samsung company?

Yes, I am.

Mr. Brown is expecting you. I'll take you up to his office. Would you get on the elevator? (knock on the door) Miss Kim is here.

Come in, please.

Please go right in.

Thank you.

D Dialogue 3   At an Office ③

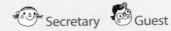 Secretary   Guest

Good afternoon.

Good afternoon. Is Mr. Jefferson in?

May I ask your name?

I am Julie of Samsung Life Insurance. Can I see him for a few minutes?

I am sorry, but may I ask you why?

I'd like to talk to him about our new insurance product.

OK. Let me see if he is available.... I'm sorry, but he is not available. Please make an appointment before you visit.

I will. Here is my business card. Please hand it to him.

Okay. Good bye.

Dialogue 4 Reception

Receptionist Guest

Front desk. Can I help you?

Yes. This is Bob Smith from room 705. Would you give me a wake-up call at six in the morning?

Certainly, sir. We'll call you at 6 a.m. tomorrow.

One more thing, there is no information in my room about making external calls.

I'm sorry. I'll ask housekeeping to check. If you dial 9, you will get an outside line.

Good. Thank you.

You're welcome. Enjoy your stay.

✿ Fill in the blanks with proper words.

| business card   available   in   hand   make an appointment |

Good afternoon.

Good afternoon. Is Mr. Jefferson _____?

May I ask your name?

I am Julie of Samsung Life Insurance. Can I see him for a few minutes?

I am sorry, but may I ask you why?

I'd like to talk to him about our new insurance product.

OK. Let me see if he is _____ ... I'm sorry, but he is not available. Please _____ before you visit.

I will. Here is my _____. Please _____ it to him.

Okay. Good bye.

Comprehension Check-up

Answer the following sentences.

1. How may I help you?

➥ _____

2. Would you get on the elevator?

➥ _____

3. May I ask your name?

➥ _____

4. May I ask you why?

➥ _____

5. Would you give me a wake-up call at 6 a.m.?

➥ _____

Translation

Translate the following sentences into English.

1. 예약하셨나요?

   ➪ _____

2. 크림과 설탕을 넣은 커피주세요.

   ➪ _____

3. 여기 제 명함이 있습니다.

   ➪ _____

4. 이유를 물어봐도 되겠습니까?

   ➪ _____

5. 방문하기 전에 약속을 잡아주세요.

   ➪ _____

6. 아침 6시에 모닝콜을 해주실 수 있습니까?

   ➪ _____

7. 즐겁게 머물다가 가십시오.

   ➪ _____

Exercise 7

1. Martin is the new _____ to help the boss.

   (A) secret   (B) security

   (C) secretary   (D) secrete

2. I have a few questions about your car _____ policy.

   (A) appearance   (B) sure

   (C) hire   (D) insurance

3. I would like to make a long distance call to Busan but there is no
   information in my room about making _____ calls.

   (A) extra   (B) professional

   (C) external   (D) internal

4. Finally, we get a chance to explain about our new _____
   to LG Display.

   (A) good   (B) emotion

   (C) produce   (D) product

5. Please _____ your homework until the end of this week.

   (A) hand in   (B) push in

   (C) give in   (D) all in

6. Would you mind _____ the window?

(A) to open   (B) opening

(C) opened   (D) open

7. He remembers _____ to business meeting.

(A) gone   (B) go

(C) to go   (D) to going

8. Nowadays, it is difficult _____ a job.

(A) got   (B) getting

(C) get   (D) to get

9. Jerry wants _____ English fluently.

(A) speak   (B) to speak

(C) spoke   (D) to speaking

10. Tom does his best _____ the problems.

(A) to solve   (B) to solving

(C) being solved   (D) solve

Answer

1. C   2. D   3. C   4. D   5. A   6. B   7. C   8. D   9. B   10. A

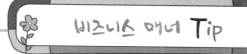

비즈니스 매너 Tip

테이블매너

기본매너

🌿 식탁에서 다리를 꼬지 않는다.

🌿 냅킨은 한 박자 쉬고 편 뒤 상단을 살짝 접은 후 무릎위에 올려놓고 식사한다.

🌿 포크와 나이프는 바깥쪽부터 안쪽 순으로 사용한다.

🌿 원형 식탁에선 빵은 왼쪽, 물은 오른쪽에 있는 것이 내 것이다.

🌿 음식물이 입안에 있을 땐 말하지 않고 입을 벌리고 씹지 않는다.

🌿 음식 먹을 때 소리를 내지 않는다.

🌿 식기류 사용 시 소리를 내지 않는다.

PART 2

Global Business English

Business English Communication

08 School Life

Key Words & Phrases

- briefly
- festival
- course
- semester
- credit
- tight
- favorite
- subject
- psychology
- interesting
- understanding
- behavior
- profession
- potluck party
- bring
- steamed pork
- yummy
- lasagna
- meatball
- pasta

Useful Expressions

1. He works part time at a restaurant.

2. He is working part time at the law firm.

3. I get along well with people.

4. Tom used to get along well with his roommate but not anymore.

5. In general, women like fancy bags, and men like fancy cars.

6. I think blood types have nothing to do with personalities.

7. It's easy to access the internet with my laptop.

8. I work on school projects with my laptop.

9. Jane is throwing a potluck party tomorrow.

10. What food are you bringing?

11. I am not good at cooking.

12. I can't wait.

13. I'm in my early 20s.

14. What do you do?

15. I am a student.

16. How many courses are you taking this semester?

17. What's your favorite subject?

D Dialogue 1   **New People**

Sunho   Julie

Hello. I'm Sunho Kim. What's your name?

My name is Julie. It's nice to meet you.

How do you spell your name?

It's J-U-L-I-E. Nice to meet you Sunho.

Where are you from, Julie?

I'm from England. How about you?

I'm from Korea but my family lives in the US.

Oh, I have to get going now. I have a class soon.

Bye for now Julie. Nice to meet you.

OK, see you.

D Dialogue 2   Introducing Yourself

Tom   Sumi

Hello. I'm Tom Johnson. You can call me Tom.

My name is Sumi Kim. You can call me Sumi.

My major is Computer Science. What do you major in?

I'm majoring in Automobile Engineering.

How are you enjoying school life?

It's so much fun. We are having the school festival next week.

Are you taking part in any events?

My classmates will run a bar at the campus. We will sell food, play games, and even have a speed-dating event during the festival.

Sounds fun. I hope you have a good time.

D Dialogue 3 At Campus

Tim   Sally

Sally! How many courses are you taking this semester?

I'm taking 7 courses. They are 19 credits in total.

You must have a tight schedule. What's your favorite subject?

I'm in love with my psychology class.

Is it fun?

It's very interesting. I want to get an understanding of the human mind and behavior.

Do you ever skip classes or arrive late?

No. I'm always on time!

D Dialogue 4 Potluck Party

 Jack Carol

Jane is throwing a potluck party tomorrow. Are you going?

Sure. What food are you bringing?

I am not good at cooking, so I ordered some steamed pork and salad.

Sounds yummy. I'll bring some lasagna and meatball pasta.

Wow. I'll be able to eat like a horse.

Me too. I can't wait.

Fill in the blanks with proper words.

briefly	run	much	part	do

Jane, can you tell me about yourself _____?

Sure. My full name is Jane Jungyeon Kim, and I'm in my early 20s.

What do you _____?

I'm a student.

How are you enjoying school life?

It's so _____ fun. We are having the school festival next week.

Are you taking _____ in any events?

My classmates will _____ a bar at the campus. We will sell food, play games, and even have a speed-dating event during the festival.

Sounds fun. I hope you have a good time.

Comprehension Check-up

🌼 Answer the following sentences.

1. May I have your name, please?

   ✍ _____

2. What do you do?

   ✍ _____

3. What's the purpose of your visit to Korea?

   ✍ _____

4. How are you enjoying school life?

   ✍ _____

5. Are you taking part in the school festival next week?

   ✍ _____

6. How many courses are you taking this semester?

   ✍ _____

7. What's your favorite subject?

   ✍ _____.

Translation

✿ Translate the following sentences into English.

1. 그는 식당에서 시간제로 일을 한다.

   ⇨ _____

2. 나는 사람들과 잘 어울려 지낸다.

   ⇨ _____

3. 나는 노트북 컴퓨터로 학교 과제를 한다.

   ⇨ _____

4. 나는 20대 초반이다.

   ⇨ _____

5. 너는 정말 빡빡한 일정을 가지고 있다.

   ⇨ _____

6. 너는 무슨 음식을 가지고 올래?

   ⇨ _____

7. 나는 요리를 잘 못한다.

   ⇨ _____

Grammar Test 1 (Word Forms)

Choose the best form to fill the gap.

1. We would like to know _____ when the program begins.

(A) exacted   (B) exactness   (C) exactly   (D) exacting

2. Please let us know your _____ time of arrival.

(A) estimated   (B) estimating   (C) estimation   (D) estimate

3. Cultural attitudes can _____ the success of a merger with an overseas firm.

(A) affectively   (B) affected   (C) affective   (D) affect

4. He _____ managed to schedule a luncheon appointment with the president.

(A) finale   (B) finally   (C) finalize   (D) final

5. The store is known for the high _____ of its products.

(A) quality   (B) qualify   (C) qualified   (D) qualification

Answer

1. C   2. A   3. D   4. B   5. A

Grammar Test 2 (Word Choice)

⚙ Choose the best form to fill the gap.

1. Computers solve problems by _____ data.

   (A) dealing   (B) meet   (C) processing   (D) affect

2. The rate of exchange _____ from day to day.

   (A) abide   (B) fluctuates   (C) related   (D) chance

3. The contract is said to be _____ of millions of dollars.

   (A) cost   (B) price   (C) value   (D) worthy

4. The company was _____ bankrupt after two years of operation.

   (A) filed   (B) called   (C) founded   (D) declared

5. Marry will have to _____ the meeting because of a previous engagement.

   (A) miss   (B) avoid   (C) arrive   (D) devoid

Answer

1. C   2. B   3. D   4. D   5. A

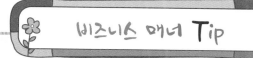

비즈니스 매너 Tip

팁 문화

일반기준

🌿 팁 문화는 서비스를 해준 사람들에 고마움을 표시하는 행위이므로 해당국가의

　일반적인 기준에 따라 적용하는 것이 좋다.

🌿 식당 : 음식 값의 15 ~ 20%

🌿 호텔 : 1~ 2달러

🌿 택시 : 요금의 10 ~ 15%

🌿 발렛파킹(valet parking) : 1~ 2달러

Chapter 09 Job Interview

Key Words & Phrases

- graduate
- national
- civil
- schedule
- dress up
- experience
- department store
- major
- application
- decide
- position
- general manager
- licence
- qualification
- certificate
- overseas
- concern
- welfare
- hands-on
- contribute

Useful **Expressions**

1. What are you going to do after you graduate?

2. I'm preparing for the national civil service exam.

3. What do you think you'll be in 5 years?

4. I want to be a government official.

5. Could you tell me about yourself?

6. I graduated from Kookje University.

7. My major is airline service.

8. What year are you in?

9. I am in the 2nd year.

10. Would you tell me your name?

11. What made you decide to apply for our company?

12. Do you have any qualifications?

13. What do you think of your personality?

14. I get along with others.

15. What do you know about our company?

16. Please tell me what you think a job is.

17. What is your vision for this job?

18. Have you had any opportunities to travel overseas?

19. I took a backpacking trip in Europe.

20. I have an associate degree.

Dialogue 1

Taeho Sumi

What will you do after college graduation?

Well, I'm preparing for the national civil service exam. What about you?

I'm scheduled for an interview at a company next week.

Sounds good.

I've got to do well at the interview. Do you have any tips?

First, I think you have to dress up for the interview.

I'm going to wear a suit and tie.

Good idea!

Dialogue 2

Personnel Manager Taeho

Good morning. Take a seat, please.

Thanks.

Could you tell me about yourself briefly?

My name is Taeho Kim. I graduated from Kookje University.

What about your work experience?

I worked as a shop master at a department store for a year.

How was it at the department store?

I liked it a lot. But I want to use my major at this company.

Well, thank you for your application.

D Dialogue 3

 Personnel Manager Taeho

Would you tell me your name?

Taeho Kim.

What made you decide to apply for this position?

Well, I wanted to get a job where I can use my major.

Do you have any licences or qualifications?

Yes. I have a certificate of overseas tour escort.

What do you think of your personality?

I am outgoing and I like to mix with people.

All right. Mr. Kim. Thanks for coming.

Dialogue 4

 Personnel Manager Applicant

What do you know about our company?

I heard that your company is very concerned about employees' welfare.

Why should we hire you?

As you have seen on my resume, my hands-on experience and educational background, I can contribute to your company.

Please tell me what you think a job is.

A job is not only a way to make a living, but also a way to contribute to society.

The interview is over. We'll call you when we decide.

⚙ Fill in the blanks with proper words.

tell	certificate	personality	apply	mix	be

Would you _____ me your name?

Tae-ho Kim.

What made you decide to _____ for this position?

Well, I wanted to get a job where I can use my major. And my goal is to _____ a general manager of a hotel in the future.

Do you have any licences or qualifications?

Yes. I have a _____ of overseas tour escort.

What do you think of your _____?

I am outgoing and I like to _____ with people.

All right. Mr. Kim. Thanks for coming.

Comprehension Check-up

 Answer the following sentences.

1. Could you tell me about yourself briefly?

   ➯ _____

2. Do you have any work experience?

   ➯ _____

3. What do you plan to do after college graduation?

   ➯ _____

4. What do you think of your personality?

   ➯ _____

5. Why do you think we should hire you?

   ➯ _____

6. Why do you think you need a job?

   ➯ _____

7. What made you decide to apply for this position?

   ➯ _____.

Translation

✿ Translate the following sentences into English.

1. 자신을 간단히 소개해 보세요.

   ⇨ _____

2. 나는 다음 주에 면접계획이 잡혀 있다

   ⇨ _____

3. 너는 정장을 차려입어야 한다.

   ⇨ _____

4. 내 꿈은 호텔 총지배인이 되는 것이다.

   ⇨ _____

5. 우리 회사에 대해 아는 것이 무엇입니까?

   ⇨ _____

6. 우리 회사는 사원의 복지에 매우 신경을 씁니다.

   ⇨ _____

7. 직업은 생계를 위한 것이다.

   ⇨ _____

Grammar Test 3 (Tense)

✿ Choose the best form to fill the gap.

1. Ms. Kim was _____ from jet lag when she returned on Saturday.

   (A) suffer   (B) suffered   (C) suffers   (D) suffering

2. Housing costs _____ substantially last year.

   (A) to rise   (B) rose   (C) have risen   (D) rising

3. He recommended that we _____ next week to discuss contract terms.

   (A) meet   (B) will meet   (3) met   (D) have met

4. The consultant suggested that the company _____ all its files to save time.

   (A) will computerize   (B) computerizes

   (C) computerized   (D) computerize

5. It is important that students _____ at least 80% of the lecture.

   (A) attends   (B) attend   (C) attended   (D) will attend

Answer

1. D   2. B   3. A   4. D   5. B

Grammar Test 4 (Passive)

Choose the best form to fill the gap.

1. Mr. Kim is _____ among his colleagues as a very generous man.

   (A) knew   (B) know   (C) knowing   (D) known

2. Of all the information on the internet, 90% _____ in English.

   (A) is stored   (B) storing   (C) have stored   (D) was storing

3. Next week, new computer systems will _____ in the office.

   (A) be installing   (B) have installed   (C) be installed   (D) was installing

4. The secretarial position _____ experience and computer skills.

   (A) is required   (B) requires   (C) requiring   (D) to require

5. All of a sudden the lights went out while the audience _____ watching a musical.

   (A) is   (B) being   (C) was   (D) been

Answer

1. D   2. A   3. C   4. B   5. C

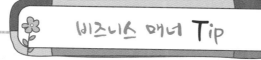

자동차 승차예절 1

운전기사가 있을 때

🍃 탈 때는 윗사람부터, 내릴 때는 반대순서로

🍃 상석순서는 첫 번째 상석은 조수석 뒷자리이고

🍃 두 번째 상석은 운전석 뒷자리

🍃 세 번째 상석은 조수석

Jobs

Key Words & Phrases

- personnel
- advertisement

- available
- part time

- full time
- receptionist

- Vietnam
- important

- deal
- jetlag

- pretty
- though

- pressure
- gym

- cashier
- leave

- while
- stressed

- work out
- hear

Useful Expressions

1. I'm calling about the ad in the newspaper.

2. Is it a part time job?

3. What are the working hours?

4. Have you ever worked at a hotel?

5. We're looking for someone with experience.

6. What's up?

7. Does everything go well?

8. I have the jetlag.

9. I have a lot of things to do.

10. My boss keeps asking me to come up with new ideas.

11. You must be under lots of pressure.

12. What do you do when you're stressed out?

13. I go for a drive in the country.

14. I go to the gym to work out.

15. I'm glad to hear you are happy.

Dialogue 1

 Authorized Personnel   Applicant

Personnel department. How may I help you?

I'm calling about the ad that I saw in the newspaper.
Is the position still available?

Yes, it is.

Is it a part time or a full time job?

It is a full time job.

What are the working hours?

It is from 9 a.m. to 5 p.m.
Have you ever worked as a hotel receptionist?

No, but I'm very kind and friendly.

I'm sorry. but we're looking for someone with experience.

Dialogue 2

 Colleague Jane

What's up, Jane?

I just got back from a business trip to Vietnam.

Did everything go well?

Yeah, I made an important business deal.

Oh, you must be happy, but you look sad.

I'm not sad. I just feel tired.

Why do you feel tired?

Because I have the jetlag.

D Dialogue 3

Colleague   Cathy

How is everything going, Cathy?

Pretty good. I have a lot to do, though.
My boss keeps asking me to come up with new ideas all the time.

You must be under lots of pressure.

Yeah, so I need to get away from work for a while.

What do you do when you're stressed out?

I usually go for a drive in the country. How about you?

Well, I usually go to the gym to work out.

You do? Good for you.

 Dialogue 4

 Cathy David

Hi, David! I haven't seen you for a while. How are you doing?

I'm OK. How about you? Are you still working at Oricom?

I changed jobs.

Why did you leave Oricom?

My work at Oricom was so hard. I got a new job as a cashier.

How do you like your new job?

For now, I like it very much.

I'm glad to hear you are happy with your new job.

Fill in the blanks with proper words.

| or | worked | but | are | newspaper | available |

Personnel department. How may I help you?

I'm calling about the ad that I saw in the _____.
Is the position still _____?

Yes, it is.

Is it a part time _____ a full time job?

It is a full time job.

What _____ the working hours?

It is from 9 a.m. to 5 p.m.
Have you ever _____ as a hotel receptionist?

No, but I'm very kind and friendly.

I'm sorry. _____ we're looking for someone with experience.

Comprehension Check-up

Answer the following sentences.

1. Why do you look so tired?

   ↪ _____

2. What do you do when you're stressed out?

   ↪ _____

3. How do you like your new job?

   ↪ _____

4. What are the working hours?

   ↪ _____

5. How are things going?

   ↪ _____

6. Do you have any work experience?

   ↪ _____

Translation

✿ Translate the following sentences into English.

1. 그 일자리가 아직 비어 있나요?

   ⇨ _____

2. 우리는 경험 있는 사람을 찾고 있습니다.

   ⇨ _____

3. 나는 시차로 인한 피로를 갖고 있다.

   ⇨ _____

4. 나는 새로운 아이디어를 찾아내야한다

   ⇨ _____

5. 나는 보통 운동하러 체육관에 다닌다.

   ⇨ _____

6. 나는 너를 본지 오래만이다.

   ⇨ _____

7. 네가 새로운 직업에 만족한다니 기쁘다.

   ⇨ _____

Grammar Test 5 (Participle)

✿ Choose the best form to fill the gap.

1. The man _____ basketball is my brother.

   (A) play   (B) playing   (C) plays   (D) have played

2. The new equipment _____ from China will be on sale next week.

   (A) is shipped   (B) shipping   (C) ships   (D) shipped

3. The sales staff should be more polite when _____ with angry customers.

   (A) deal   (B) to dealing   (C) dealt   (D) dealing

4. Please visit the baggage services booth for more information regarding lost or _____ baggage.

   (A) damages   (B) damaged   (C) damage   (D) damaging

5. The _____ catalogue prices are effective as from February 15.

   (A) revised   (B) revising   (C) revises   (D) revision

✎ **A**nswer

1. B   2. D   3. D   4. B   5. A

Grammar Test 6 (Gerund)

⚙ Choose the best form to fill the gap.

1. After he apologized for _____, he sat at the back of the classroom.

   (A) later   (B) lately   (C) being late   (D) latest

2. The product was good enough _____ our high standards.

   (A) satisfy   (B) satisfying   (C) to satisfying   (D) to satisfy

3. We enjoyed _____ a walk in the morning daily.

   (A) take   (B) taking   (C) to take   (D) taken

4. We look forward _____ you at your earliest convenience.

   (A) to meet   (B) to meeting   (C) meeting   (D) meet

5. The grass cutter stopped _____ because the battery was dead.

   (A) work   (B) to work   (C) working   (D) worked

Answer

1. C   2. D   3. B   4. B   5. C

자동차 승차예절 2

상사가 운전할 때

🌱 첫 번째 상석은 운전석

🌱 두 번째 상석은 조수석

🌱 세 번째 상석은 조수석 뒷자리

🌱 네 번째 상석은 운전석 뒷자리

하급자가 운전할 때

🌱 첫 번째 상석은 조수석 뒷자리

🌱 두 번째 상석은 운전석 뒷자리

🌱 세 번째 상석은 조수석

Complaints

Key Words & Phrases

- photocopies
- printer
- manager

- replace
- machine
- jammed

- laptop
- order
- receive

- problem
- suppliers
- cancel

- send
- afraid
- infected

- wrong
- access
- download

- anti-virus
- show up
- compatible

- complaint
- problem
- air-conditioning

- reserve
- double
- moment

Useful Expressions

1. Could you make 10 photocopies of this article?

2. The laptop is not working properly.

3. The copy machine is jammed again.

4. I will have to cancel it if I don't receive it tomorrow.

5. I'm sorry for the delay.

6. My computer is infected with a virus.

7. I will see what I can do.

8. We are sorry for the inconvenience.

9. You must download a compatible viewer.

10. This is Ms. Jung in room 903.

11. I have a complaint about my room.

12. The air-conditioning doesn't work.

13. I'll send someone up right away.

14. I reserved a single room, not a double room.

15. I'm sorry. I'll talk to the manager.

16. We haven't received the price list yet.

17. I hope we can iron this out quickly.

18. I am seriously considering legal action.

19. We will reship the products via air freight at our expense.

20. It's against company policy to give refunds.

Dialogue 1

 Kevin Carol

Could you make 10 photocopies of this article for the meeting?

I'm sorry, but this printer is out of order.

Why don't you ask the manager to make it replaced?

I did. But the copy machine is jammed again.

What should I do? They should be ready by tomorrow.

Don't worry. I can print it out at the next office.

Thanks.

Dialogue 2

 Service Department Jungmin

Service department. May I help you?

I'm calling about my order for the laptop. I placed the order about two weeks ago. But I haven't received it yet.

Sorry for the delay. Could I have your name?

I'm Jungmin Lee.

I'm very sorry. We have had some problems with our suppliers.

I will have to cancel if I don't receive it by the end of this month.

I'm sorry again. We will be able to send the laptop as soon as possible.

I see. Thanks.

Dialogue 3

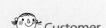 Customer  Service Department

I'm afraid that my computer is infected with a virus.

What's wrong with the computer?

I cannot access the internet.

I think you should download an anti-virus program.

Now I open up a file, but it doesn't show up.

You have to install a compatible viewer.

How can I do that?

You must download a compatible viewer from the internet.

Dialogue 4

 Ms. Jung  Front Desk Clerk

Hello. This is Ms. Jung in room 1005.

Front Desk. How can I help you?

I have a complaint about my room.

I'm very sorry. What's the problem?

Well, the air-conditioning doesn't work.

Oh, no. I'll send someone up right away.

And there is another thing. I reserved a single room, not a double.

Just a moment, please. I'll talk to the manager.

Fill in the blanks with proper words.

| send | have | with | about | cancel | placed |

Service department. May I help you?

I'm calling _____ my order for the laptop. I _____ the order about two weeks ago. But I haven't received it yet.

Sorry for the delay. Could I _____ your name?

I'm Jungmin Lee.

I'm very sorry. We have had some problems _____ our suppliers.

I will have to _____ if I don't receive it by the end of this month.

I'm sorry again. We will be able to _____ the laptop as soon as possible.

I see. Thanks.

Comprehension Check-up

✿ Answer the following sentences.

1. Could you make 10 photocopies of this article?

   ➪ _____

2. Did you ask the maintenance to make it fixed?

   ➪ _____

3. I'm calling about the laptop I ordered a week ago.

   ➪ _____

4. What's wrong with your computer?

   ➪ _____

5. How can I install a compatible viewer?

   ➪ _____

6. Front desk. How can I help you?

   ➪ _____

7. I'm very sorry. What's the problem?

   ➪ _____.

Translation

Translate the following sentences into English.

1. 복사기가 막혀서 꼼짝도 안합니다.

   ⇨ _____

2. 우리의 공급자에게 문제가 있었습니다.

   ⇨ _____

3. 나는 인터넷에 접근할 수 없다.

   ⇨ _____

4. 나는 1005호에 머물고 있는 미스터 김입니다.

   ⇨ _____

5. 내 방에 문제가 있습니다.

   ⇨ _____

6. 사람을 올려 보내겠습니다.

   ⇨ _____

7. 잠시만 기다리세요. 매니저와 상의해 보겠습니다.

   ⇨ _____

Grammar Test 7 (Infinitive)

⚙ Choose the best form to fill the gap.

1. He will talk about what employees should do in order _____ _____ their productivity.

   (A) improve   (B) improving   (C) to improving   (D) to improve

2. The economy is expected _____ within a few months.

   (A) improve   (B) improving   (C) to improve   (D) improved

3. Julie went to Seoul _____ with the president of ABC company.

   (A) for meeting   (B) for meet   (C) to meet   (D) meeting

4. It is important _____ all these directions completely.

   (A) to following   (B) following   (C) to follow   (D) follow

5. _____ is possible for robots to carry out several tasks at the same time.

   (A) that   (B) it   (C) this   (D) there

Answer

1. D   2. C   3. C   4. C   5. B

Grammar Test 8 (Pronoun)

⚙ Choose the best form to fill the gap.

1. Linda convinced _____ boss to accept the offer.

   (A) hers   (B) her   (C) she   (D) herself

2. _____ difficult to get tickets for such a popular show.

   (A) There are   (B) They are   (C) It is   (D) There is

3. The board of directors announced that _____ would open a new branch soon.

   (A) they   (B) their   (C) them   (D) themselves

4. The company invited the public to see _____ new facilities.

   (A) it   (B) its   (C) them   (D) theirs

5. They did not come, even though we had sent _____ an invitation.

   (A) them   (B) their   (C) themselves   (D) theirs

✏ **Answer**

1. B   2. C   3. A   4. B   5. A

인사 매너 1

목례(눈인사)

🍃 서로 눈을 보고 가볍게 고개 숙이는 인사로 5°정도 숙인다.

🍃 실내에서 자주 마주쳤을 때

🍃 상대방이 대화중 또는 식사중일 때

🍃 엘리베이터, 화장실 등 여러 사람이 이용하는 장소에서 마주쳤을 때

🍃 모르는 사람과 마주쳤을 때

12 Office Works

Key Words & Phrases

- supply room
- favor
- document
- save
- network
- share
- care
- sandwich
- certainly
- presentation
- fingerprint
- sensor
- Tuesday
- prepare
- slide
- create
- Saturday
- finish
- typo
- complete
- staff
- luncheon
- appointment
- stockholder
- schedule
- hand-out
- social
- light
- refreshment
- ready

Useful Expressions

1. Where can I find paper sheet?

2. Where is the supply room?

3. Do you know where the files are?

4. Could you do me a favor?

5. Could you print out ten copies of this documents?

6. Can you get a sandwich for me?

7. Could you help me prepare the presentation?

8. Could you please create Power Point slides?

9. Until when do I have to create it?

10. Can you finish it until this Saturday?

11. Can you tell me what my schedule is today?

12. When is the stockholder's meeting scheduled?

13. Could you make 7 copies this article?

14. We are going to have a social time.

15. I'll have some light refreshments ready.

Dialogue 1

 Sam Ellen

Excuse me. Where can I find paper sheet?

They're in the supply room.

Where is the supply room?

The supply room is the next room.

Do you know where the files are?

Why don't you check the file cabinet? They should be there.

Thank you very much.

Dialogue 2

Sam   Ellen

Could you do me a favor?

Sure. What is it?

Could you print out ten copies of this document? I have it saved on a network share.

I'll take care of it right away.

And can you get a sandwich for me? I don't have time to go out for lunch today.

Certainly. I'd be happy to.

Dialogue 3

 Sam  Ellen

I am due to give a presentation on our new fingerprint sensor next Tuesday. Could you please help me prepare the presentation?

Sure. I'd be happy to.

Could you please create Power Point slides?

Yes, I will. Until when do I have to create it?

At least until this Saturday. Can you finish it in time?

Yes, I think I can.

Please make no typos. When you complete it, please email it to me.

Yes, I will.

Dialogue 4

Sam Ellen

Ellen, can you tell me what my schedule is today?

You have a staff meeting at 9 a.m. and a luncheon appointment with Mike at noon.

When is the stockholder's meeting scheduled?

It is scheduled next Saturday at 2 p.m.

I see. This is a handout for staff meeting.
Could you please make seven copies of it?

Yes, anything else?

We are going to have a social time with light refreshments after the meeting.

I'll have them ready.

Fill in the blanks with proper words.

| make | handout | luncheon | scheduled | else | refreshments |

Ms. kim. can you tell me what my schedule is today?

You have a staff meeting at 9 a.m. and a _____ appointment with Mike at noon.

When is the stockholder's meeting _____?

It is scheduled next Saturday at 2 p.m.

I see. This is a _____ for staff meeting.

Could you please _____ 7 copies of it?

Yes, anything _____?

We are going to have a social time with light _____ after the meeting.

I'll have them ready.

Comprehension Check-up

 Answer the following sentences.

1. Where can I find paper sheet?

   ⇨ _____

2. Could you do me a favor?

   ⇨ _____

3. Could you print out ten copies of this document?

   ⇨ _____

4. Can you get a sandwich for me?

   ⇨ _____

5. Could you make seven copies of this handout?

   ⇨ _____

6. Can you finish it until this Saturday?

   ⇨ _____

7. Would you prepare some refreshments for the meeting?

   ⇨ _____ .

Translation

❀ Translate the following sentences into English.

1. 인쇄지가 어디에 있나요?

   ➪ _____

2. 부탁을 드려도 될까요?

   ➪ _____

3. 지금 바로 하겠습니다.

   ➪ _____

4. 시간 내에 그것을 마칠 수 있나요?

   ➪ _____

5. 오타가 있으면 안 됩니다.

   ➪ _____

6. 오늘 정오에 오찬 약속이 있습니다.

   ➪ _____

7. 회의를 위해 약간의 다과를 준비하겠습니다.

   ➪ _____

Grammar Test 9 (Adjective)

✿ Choose the best form to fill the gap.

1. I don't have _____ money to cover the bill.

   (A) too much   (B) enough   (C) so many   (D) exactly

2. The cost of living is _____ in London than in Seoul.

   (A) high   (B) highly   (C) higher   (D) highest

3. The advantage of this project is that it is twice as _____ as the other.

   (A) cheap   (B) cheaper   (C) cheapest   (D) cheaply

4. Of all the two candidates, Mr. Lee is the _____.

   (A) good   (B) well   (C) better   (D) best

5. Tom spent a _____ amount of money on the purchase of the house.

   (A) consideration   (B) considerate   (c) considering   (D) considerable

Answer

   1. B   2. C   3. A   4. C   5. D

Grammar Test 10 (Adverb)

⚙ Choose the best form to fill the gap.

1. By the end of the day, _____ all of the orders had been shipped.

   (A) near   (B) nearing   (C) nearly   (D) nearby

2. If you _____ watch many problems in society, you can find solutions to them.

   (A) close   (B) closing   (C) closed   (D) closely

3. The seminar began _____ after the manager left the office.

   (A) briefly   (B) shortly   (C) sooner   (D) rightly

4. The venture company launched the _____ designed product.

   (A) renewal   (B) newer   (C) newly   (D) new

5. The manager has _____ decided how to cope with the new problems.

   (A) already   (B) yet   (C) once   (D) always

✏ **Answer**

1. C   2. D   3. B   4. C   5. A

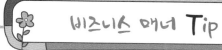

인사 매너 2

보통 인사

🌿 상체를 30° 정도 숙인다.

🌿 일반적으로 가장 기본이 되는 인사이다.

🌿 윗사람이나 내방객을 만나거나 헤어질 때

🌿 고객을 접대할 때

13 Chapter Business Trip

Key Words & Phrases

- customs
- declare
- souvenir

- invoice
- stay
- purpose

- airport
- limousine
- outside

- entrance
- pressed
- helpful

- mention
- due
- accident

- heard
- serious
- appreciate

- join
- pick up
- tech

- company
- product
- interest

- catalogue

Useful Expressions

1. Do you have anything to declare?

2. All I have are some souvenirs.

3. Do you have an invoice?

4. How long are you going to stay in Seoul?

5. What's the purpose of your visit to Korea?

6. I hope you have a good time.

7. Where can I take an airport limousine?

8. You had better take a subway.

9. How often does it run?

10. I'm pressed for time.

11. I'm sorry I couldn't meet you at the airport.

12. You've been very helpful.

13. Don't mention it.

14. I appreciate your understanding.

15. I'll come by and pick you up at your hotel.

16. I'll be waiting for you in the lobby.

17. Please be my guest for dinner, if you have time.

18. I'd love to join you.

19. I'm Alex of GM Company.

20. We'll get in touch with you soon.

D Dialogue 1 Customs

 Customs officer   Alex

Do you have anything to declare?

No. All I have are a few souvenirs.

Do you have an invoice for them?

Certainly, here it is.

How long are you going to stay in Seoul?

About two weeks.

What's the purpose of your visit?

For business.

Fine. I hope you have a good time.

Thank you.

D Dialogue 2 Information Desk

😊 Tourist   😊 Information Desk staff

😊 Where can I take an airport limousine?

😊 You had better take a subway outside the entrance of this building.

😊 How often does it run?

😊 Every one hour.

😊 I'm pressed for time. I guess I'll take a cab.

😊 I hope you enjoyed your stay.

😊 Thanks! You've been very helpful.

😊 Don't mention it.

Dialogue 3 — At a Hotel

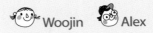
Woojin   Alex

Woojin: May I speak to Alex?

Alex: Speaking.

Woojin: This is Woojin Kim.
I'm sorry I couldn't meet you at the airport due to an accident.

Alex: I heard about it. I hope it's not serious.

Woojin: I appreciate your understanding.
Please be my guest for dinner if you are free this evening.

Alex: Thank you. I'd love to join you.

Woojin: Fine. I'll come by and pick you up at your hotel at 5.

Alex: Okay. I'll be waiting for you in the lobby.

D Dialogue 4 — A New Business Contact

 Alex   Woojin

How do you do?
I'm Alex of the GM tech company.

I'm glad to meet you. I'd like to know about your products.

We appreciate your interest. I have some catalogues for you.

Thank you. Are the prices up to date?

Of course.

Do you have any samples with you?

No, I'm afraid I don't.
But we can get them to you later.

Good. Let us look over the catalogues.
We'll get in touch with you soon.

Fill in the blanks with proper words.

better	often	take	mention	pressed

Where can I _____ an airport limousine?

You had _____ take a subway outside the entrance of this building.

How _____ does it run?

Every one hour.

I'm _____ for time. I guess I'll take a cab.

I hope you enjoyed your stay.

Thanks! You've been very helpful.

Don't _____ it.

Comprehension Check-up

⚙ Answer the following sentences.

1. Do you have anything to declare?

   ➭ _____

2. Do you have an invoice?

   ➭ _____

3. What's the purpose of your visit to Korea?

   ➭ _____

4. How long are you going to stay in Seoul?

   ➭ _____

5. I'm Alex of GM Company.

   ➭ _____

6. Do you have any samples with you?

   ➭ _____

7. Please be my guest for dinner, if you have time.

   ➭ _____.

Translation

✿ Translate the following sentences into English.

1. 내가 갖고 있는 것은 몇 개의 기념품입니다.

    ➪ _____

2. 청구서가 있습니까?

    ➪ _____

3. 방문 목적이 무엇입니까?

    ➪ _____

4. 당신은 지하철을 타는 편이 낫습니다.

    ➪ _____

5. 저녁에 호텔로 모시러 가겠습니다.

    ➪ _____

6. 가격은 최근의 것입니까?

    ➪ _____

7. 카탈로그를 살펴봅시다.

    ➪ _____

Grammar Test 11 (Prepositions)

✿ Choose the best form to fill the gap.

1. The concert began _____ 4:00.

   (A) at   (B) to   (C) for   (D) during

2. This project will be funded _____ two years.

   (A) during   (B) for   (C) since   (D) until

3. The weatherman forecasts that the weather will be sunny _____ _____ the weekend.

   (A) entire   (B) whole   (C) at   (D) throughout

4. The report predicts that prices will rise _____ 3% next month.

   (A) by   (B) from   (C) through   (D) between

5. We look forward to doing business _____ you as soon as possible.

   (A) to   (B) from   (C) about   (D) with

Answer

   1. A   2. B   3. D   4. A   5. D

Grammar Test 12 (Relative Clause)

Choose the best form to fill the gap.

1. People_____ invested in the stock believes that they will gain a large profit.

   (A) which   (B) whose   (C) what   (D) who

2. The employees _____ idea is creative will be rewarded with a $700 bonus.

   (A) which   (B) whoes   (C) whom   (D) who

3. They provided us with coupons _____ can be used at the traditional market.

   (A) whichever   (B) whatever   (C) which   (D) what

4. Steve described _____ he had seen at the Traders Expo.

   (A) that   (B) what   (C) whoes   (D) which

5. The job fair was held in the city _____ my parents lived.

   (A) how   (B) when   (C) why   (D) where

Answer

1. D   2. B   3. C   4. B   5. D

비즈니스 매너 Tip

인사 매너 3

정중한 인사

🌿 상체를 45° 정도 숙인다.

🌿 감사 또는 사과를 표시할 때

🌿 공식석상에서 처음 인사할 때

🌿 면접할 때

OPIc
(Oral Proficiency Interview-Computer)

Key Words & Phrases

✿ OPIc-컴퓨터를 통해 진행되는 iBT 기반의 외국어 말하기 평가

- process
- detail
- cook

- boil
- flake
- instant

- noodle
- add
- chop

- scallion
- depend
- minute

- dental
- clinic
- close

- scaling
- magazine
- beverage

- arrive
- destination
- tourist

- spot
- specialty
- indicate

- frequently

Useful Expressions

1. Tell me a little bit about yourself.

2. I work part-time at an wedding hall.

3. I am outgoing and sociable.

4. It takes about 40 minutes by car from my house.

5. I live in Pyeongtaek.

6. It takes about 40 minutes by car to get here.

7. What kind of food do you like to cook?

8. Can you tell me the process of making that food?

9. Which dental clinic do you usually visit?

10. I go to YE Dental Clinic in my city.

11. My favorite tourism attraction in Korea is Seorak Mountain.

12. I love going there because of its beautiful scenery.

13. It is near the ocean and mountains.

14. Jeonju City is well-known for a dish called Bibimbap.

15. This is warm rice with vegetables, red pepper paste, and an egg.

16. I try to find a famous dish like this everytime I travel.

Topic 1　Self-Introduction

Topic Question

Let's start the interview.

Tell me a little bit about yourself.

Model Answer

My name is Na-yeong Lee and I'm in my 20s.

I'm a student.

I work part-time at an wedding hall.

I am outgoing and sociable.

I guess that's why I can get along with people.

On the other hand, I live in Pyeongtaek.

Cooking

Topic Question

What kind of food do you like to cook?

Can you tell me the process of making that food?

Please tell me in detail about how you make it?

Model Answer

I like to cook ramen because it is easier to make than any other food.

First, boil some water.

Next, put in the soup base, flakes, and instant noodles.

Then, you can add an egg and some chopped scallions, depending on your personal taste.

You should boil it for about 2 minutes and then it will be ready.

Topic 3　Dental Clinic

Topic Question

Which dental clinic do you usually visit?

Why do you go to that clinic?

Give me a good description of the dental clinic that you go to.

Model Answer

I go to YE Dental Clinic in my city.

I visit this clinic because it's close to my house and the service is good.

I go to the clinic once a year to get a dental scaling.

The dentist is in his early 40s.

She is very friendly and skillful.

I feel comfortable when I visit the clinic.

The clinic has a nice waiting room with various magazines and beverages.

Topic 4 **Traveling**

Topic Question

When traveling, what do you do when you arrive at your destination?

Do you prefer to look around tourist spots or go shopping?

Or maybe you spend time in your hotel.

Please tell me about it in detail.

Model Answer

When I'm traveling, I love to try the local food.

I think this is the best way to learn about a new place.

In Korea, each region has very different types of local food.

Many places have a specialty food.

For example, Jeonju City is well-known for a dish called Bibimbap.

This is warm rice with vegetables, red pepper paste, and an egg.

Topic 5 **Favorite Tourist Spot**

Topic Question

You indicated in the survey that you like to travel around your country.

Please tell me about a city you frequently visit.

Give some details about it and tell why you like it.

Model Answer

My favorite place to travel in Korea is Sokcho City.

I love going there because of its beautiful scenery.

It is near the ocean and mountains.

It is a wonderful place to visit any time of year.

I visit famous tourist spots to see the cherry blossoms in the spring.

In the summer, it's a good place to enjoy swimming in the ocean.

In the fall, you can see the color changes of the mountains.

In the winter, I even enjoy walking on Duleagil covered with snow, which is a kind of circular road for walking.

✿ Fill in the blanks with proper words.

comfortable	with	takes	his	turn	under

I go to YE Dental Clinic in my city. I visit this clinic because it's close to

my our place and the service is good. It _____ only 10

minutes to walk there from my house.

I go to the clinic once a year to get a dental scaling. The dentist is in

_____ early 50s. He is very friendly and skillful. Once,

I had to go _____ anesthesia to have one of my wisdom

teeth pulled. But I felt little pain when he gave me a shot in my gums.

I feel _____ when I visit the clinic. The clinic has

a nice waiting room _____ various magazines and

beverages. I always pick up one of the fashion magazines there while I wait my

_____. I like that classical music plays there all the time.

Comprehension Check-up

Answer the following sentences.

1. Please tell me about a city you frequently visit.

   ⇨ _____

2. Tell me why you like it.

   ⇨ _____

3. When traveling, what do you do when you arrive at your destination?

   ⇨ _____

4. Do you prefer to look around tourist spots or go shopping?

   ⇨ _____

5. When was the last time you went to the dental clinic?

   ⇨ _____

6. Why do you go to that clinic?

   ⇨ _____

Translation

✿ Translate the following sentences into English.

1. 나는 매우 사교적인 사람이다.

   ⇨ _____

2. 당신은 계란과 약간의 다진 파를 첨가할 수 있다.

   ⇨ _____

3. 여행할 때, 나는 지역음식을 먹어보는 것을 좋아한다.

   ⇨ _____

4. 나는 이 병원이 집에서 가깝기 때문에 다닌다.

   ⇨ _____

5. 나는 아름다운 경치 때문에 거기에 가기를 좋아한다.

   ⇨ _____

6. 가을에 당신은 산에 단풍이 드는 것을 볼 수 있다.

   ⇨ _____

Grammar Test 13 (Mixed)

❀ Choose the best form to fill the gap.

1. I have some money and credit card in _____ wallet.

   (A) mine   (B) I   (C) my   (D) me

2. The girls are smart, but _____ are not wise.

   (A) they   (B) you   (C) we   (D) it

3. _____ mechanic has worked at Hyundai Auto shop for 2 years.

   (A) someone   (B) those   (C) such   (D) this

4. Merging with another company is a complicated and _____ _____ issue.

   (A) sensible   (B) sensitive   (C) sense   (D) sensual

5. All visitors to the museum must _____ the rules.

   (A) follow   (B) to follow   (C) following   (D) follows

Answer

1. C   2. A   3. D   4. B   5. A

Grammar Test 14 (Mixed)

⚙ Choose the best form to fill the gap.

1. A number of security cameras installed in the building _____ _____ 24 hours a day.

   (A) record   (B) recording   (C) records   (D) to record

2. _____ shopping online, make sure you check the expiration date.

   (A) by   (B) because of   (C) to   (D) when

3. The pressure cooker _____ ordered yesterday will be delivered tomorrow.

   (A) you   (B) your   (C) yours   (D) yourself

4. Either snow _____ rain is expected to affect the region tomorrow.

   (A) both   (B) and   (C) nor   (D) or

5. _____ yourself to the audience is the first step of your presentation.

   (A) introduction   (B) introduced   (C) introducing   (D) introduce

📖 **Answer**

1. A   2. D   3. A   4. D   5. C

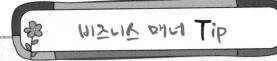

상석예절 1

연회장(Banquet hall)

🌿 상석위치는 시야 및 경치가 좋고 편안한 좌석으로 일반적으로 출입구에서

떨어진 쪽이다.

🌿 주빈석(head table)은 연단에서 제일 가까운 열의 중앙 테이블이고

대개 출입구에서 제일 먼 쪽이 된다.

🌿 이 테이블에서 제일 상석(place of honor)은 무대가 잘 보이고 무대와

마주 보는 좌석이다.

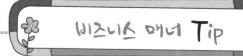

비즈니스 매너 Tip

상석예절 2

회의실

🌿 출입구 반대 측이 상석이다. 그리고 상석에서 멀어질수록 말석이다.

🌿 스크린이 있을 시 화면을 마주보는 쪽이 상석이다.

응접실

🌿 소파(sofa, 긴 의자)가 개별의자보다 상석 서열이 높다.

🌿 의자가 적게 놓인 곳이 상석 서열이 높다.

Cover Letter

Sumi Kim
#102-1005 Woolim Apt.
Hannam-dong, Yongsan-gu
Seoul, Korea

March, 12th, 2018

Personnel Dept.
SD Tech
1-23 Guro-dong, Guro-gu
Seoul, Korea

To whom it may concern:

I'm writing to apply for the position of engineer as advertised in the daily newspaper.
I expect to receive a Bachalor of Science degree in Computer Engineering in Februery. I have been a programmer trainee in the engineering department at Samsung for 6 months and have gained a good deal of experience in computer applications.

I'll be happy to meet with you at your convenience and discuss how my education and experience will suit your needs. You can reach me at my cell phone, at 010-3445-5789, or at kooky@naver.com.

Sincerely yours.

Sumi Kim
Sumi Kim

Enclosure : resume

Resume

Personal Data

Name : Joon Ho Lee

Date of birth : June 7th, 1997

Current Address : #102-1005, DB Apt., Seocho-Dong 546, Seocho-Gu, Seoul, Korea

Tel : 010-3445-2345

Joonho67@naver.com

Objective

A position as a secretary with opportunities to use computer skills

Education

2016-2018 Graduated from Dept. of Computer Information & Communication, Kookje University (Associate Degree)

2013-2016 Seoul High School

Work Experience

2018 Present Sales Manager, SK T-world

Skills

Computer : Word Processing Skills 1st Class

Language : Basic Conversation in English

References : Available on Request

Business Letter

ABC Company
123 Main Street
LA, CA 13520
Tel: (533) 422 1350

January 2, 2018

Kookje Hotel
45 Jangahn Dong
Pyeongtaek, Kyonggido

Dear Sir or Madam:

I would like to request some information about your hotel. I'm planning to stay at your hotel from February 2 to February 5. Do you have a suite available for the period? I would also like to know what the cost would be.

Please don't hesitate to call me. Good luck with everything.

Sincerely yours,

_____

Chris
Sales Manager
ABC Company

Business Letter Structure

1. Letter head/Sender's address	보내는 사람 주소
2. Date	날짜
3. Inside address	받는 사람 주소
4. Salutation	_____ 귀하
5. Message	메시지
6. Closing	끝맺음
7. Sincerely yours,	
8. Signature	푸른색 펜
9. Printed name and position	보내는 사람의 이름과 직위

Position at the Company

- 대리 : assistant manager
- 과장 : manager
- 차장 : deputy general manager
- 부장 : general manager
- 이사 : executive director
- 상무 : managing director
- 전무 : senior managing director
- 부사장 : executive vice president
- 사장 : president
- 부회장 : vice-chaiman
- 회장 : chaiman
- 최고 경영자(CEO) : chief executive officer

Sentence Pattern

● 동사형

1. S+V: Birds sing./ The sun is shining brightly

2. S+V+adv: He came in./ I get up at six.

3. S+V+p+n: He came into the room./ This house belongs to my father.

4. S+V+C: This is mine./ I feel unwell.

5. S+V+as+C: He acted as interpreter.

6. S+V+O: Everybody loves her./ I bought the book yesterday.

7. S+V+O+adv: She took her hat off./ He has brought about her ruin.

8. S+V+to do: He wants to see you./ They seem to be happy.

9. S+V+wh. to do: I don't know what to do.

10. S+V+doing: He stopped walking./ She stood waiting for me.

11. S+V+that clause: He said that you should go there.

12. S+V+wh. clause: Do you know where he lives?

13. S+V+O+p+n: They furnished us with some clothes.

14. S+V+O+O: She gave them the apples.

15. S+V+O+that clause: I told him that he was mistaken.

16. S+V+O+wh- clause: I asked the guide when the tower had been built.

17: S+V+O+wh- to do: The policeman showed me how to get there.

18: S+V+O+C: They elected him President./ The sun keeps us warm.

19: S+V+O+as+C: We regard him as a danger to society.

20: S+V+O+p.p: I will have my watch repaired.

21: S+V+O+doing: I heard a dog barking.

22: S+V+O+to do: We cannot allow the boys to play baseball here.

23: S+V+O+V: Let them come in.

● 명사형

1. + to do: He has the ability to do the task.

2. + p+doing: I have the pleasure of speaking to you.

3. + that clause: The idea that you should help her did not please me.

4. +(p+)wh-절.구: I was in doubt (about) whether to believe it or not.

● 형용사형

1. + to do: He was able to do the task.

2. + p+doing: She was capable of fulfilling all promises.

3. + of + n+ to do: It's kind of you to bring it to me.

4. + that clause: I am glad that you have succeeded.

5. + (p+)wh- 절.구: He was anxious (about) how you got on.

Proverbs

1. You never owned anything except your MOMENTS.

   Every Moment you lived was yours.

   Life is just a Moment.

   Live it...

   Love it...

   Enjoy it...

2. What is important is to keep learning, to enjoy challenge, and to tolerate ambiguity. In the end there is no answers.

3. Our aim should be service, not success.

4. Whatever you do, do cautiously, and look to the end.

5. He who has never hoped can never despair. There is only meaningless suffering.

6. Chance favors only the prepared mind.

7. If I have lost confidence in myself, I have the universe against me.

8. I haven't failed, I've found 10,000 ways that don't work.

9. In everything, do to others what you would have them do to you.

10. Those who leave everything in God's hand will eventually see God's hand in everything.

11. You must sow before you can reap.

12. Stay Hungry, Stay Foolish.

13. The best is yet to come.

14. Cast a cold eye on Life, on Death. Horseman, pass by!

15. I knew if I stayed around long enough, something like this would happen.

16. It shall also come to pass.

17. Where there's a will, there's a way.

18. A man's character is his fate.

19. Life's greatest happiness is to be convinced we are loved.

20. The man who doesn't read good books has no advantage over the man who can't read them.

21. Without hope, there is no despair. There is only meaningless suffering.

22. Breathe. Let go. And remind yourself that this very moment is the only one you know you have for sure.

23. The riper the grain is, the lower it hangs its head.

24. Ask, and it will be given to you. Seek, and you will find it. Knock, and the door will be opened.

비즈니스 매너의 기본요소

기본요소

🌿 단정한 용모와 복장

🌿 밝은 인사

🌿 반듯한 자세

🌿 미소 띤 온화한 표정

🌿 바르고 고운 말씨

저자소개

정은주(Eun Joo Jeong)
세종대학교 대학원 영문학 박사
현) 국제대학교 호텔관광과 교수

고인숙(Inn Sook Koh)
성균관대학교 영어영문학과 졸업
현) 국제대학교 컴퓨터정보통신과 교수

김철진(Chul Jin Kim)
성균관대학교 전자공학과 졸업
현) 국제대학교 컴퓨터정보통신과 교수
전) 삼성전자 전무, 삼성전자 미국연구법인장 역임

Global Business English

초판 1쇄 인쇄   2018년 3월   5일
초판 1쇄 발행   2018년 3월 10일

저 자	정은주 · 고인숙 · 김철진
펴낸이	임 순 재
펴낸곳	**(주)한올출판사**
등 록	제11-403호
주 소	서울시 마포구 모래내로 83(성산동 한올빌딩 3층)
전 화	(02) 376-4298(대표)
팩 스	(02) 302-8073
홈페이지	www.hanol.co.kr
e-메 일	hanol@hanol.co.kr
ISBN	979-11-5685-635-1